CRIMINALS AND LAW ENFORCERS IN TV ENTERTAINMENT

PRIME TIME CRIME

A Study by
Linda S. Lichter and S. Robert Lichter

With a Foreword by Leonard J. Theberge

the media institute

Table of Contents

Foreword

When Edith Bunker announced to her husband, Archie, and 20 million viewers of *All in the Family* that she had been raped, television took a dramatic turn toward realism. Norman Lear and his fellow Hollywood producers felt it was time to present the television viewing audience with three-dimensional characters acting out their lives in a real and dangerous world.

No longer would TV characters, portrayed by the likes of Lucille Ball and Dick Van Dyke, be able to avoid dealing with the harsh and unpleasant realities of crime in America. Nor would the "Joe Friday" type of cop from *Dragnet* or *Adam 12* any longer be immune to the temptations of a bribe or other serious indiscretions.

Newer programs like *Lou Grant* and *Hill Street Blues* emphasized the fallability of our public officials by placing these characters in awkward and sometimes compromising positions. And even when this new genre of TV-realism focuses on comic or fanciful characters, the encroaching threat of the "real" world is ever present as during a recent episode of *Mork and Mindy* when an elderly couple are brutally mugged.

Television producers and programmers, however, can hardly be faulted for introducing crime into programs hitherto devoid of such controversial fare. Consider, for instance, that in 1979 over 40 million Americans were victims of attempted criminal offenses, according to the National Crime Survey.

A report released in 1980 *(The Figgie Report on Fear of Crime)* found that two of every five Americans are highly fearful that they will become victims of violent crimes such as murder, rape, robbery or assault, and that even greater percentages of the population are taking a variety of rather strict security precautions. Crime is now a fact of life, even where "Father Knows Best."

But as we have pointed out in our earlier studies, "realism" TV-style rarely conforms to the reality of life—and nowhere is this more true than in television's portrayal of crime and law enforcement in America. As this study by Drs. Linda and Robert Lichter for The Media Institute shows, television may be presenting three-dimensional characters —but those characters are acting in a one-dimensional setting which bears little in common with reality.

We are struck by the findings of this study which indicate that the televised picture of crime and criminals is virtually the opposite of real life. Using the most recent FBI statistics, researchers compared actual crime figures with statistics gathered on hundreds of prime-time television episodes. The comparisons reveal disparities of such magnitude as to give one pause.

For instance, 82 percent of those arrested in 1980 for offenses which comprise the FBI Crime Index were individuals under the age of 30. But on television the vast majority of criminals are adults over 30. Despite the fact that most criminals come from impoverished backgrounds, most television criminals are portrayed as either high-class "mafia" types, businessmen or corrupt police and government officials. Murder and other violent crimes are far more likely to occur on television than in real life—12 times more frequently according to this study. However one slices the statistical pie, television crime is generally the opposite of what takes place on the streets.

One reason for this disparity may be fairly obvious: most common crimes and criminals don't make good copy. Television viewers would soon tire of shows focusing on drunkenness and petty larceny. Murder, kidnapping and espionage may comprise only a small percentage of all crimes committed, but they are the stuff of which good (i.e. action-packed) TV scripts are made. Perhaps this is why prime-time criminals are overwhelmingly wealthy and white-collar when, in reality, statistics indicate just the opposite.

But on a deeper level, perhaps this reflects a phenomenon we have noted in our earlier studies—that television programming is permeated by a strong bias against authority and institutions in our society. Men and women who exercise power, whether in business, government, unions or law enforcement, frequently are shown as waging a relentless war to oppress the "little guy".

And this demonstrates TV's corollary bias: an egalitarian preoccupation with the average guy, especially if he is an entrepreneur or otherwise outside the "Establishment". Maybe this is the reason TV's most successful law enforcers are private eyes and private citizens—and why television's most successful policemen are the ones who "bend" the rules.

At bottom, however, we are left with the perplexing question: what effect do these distorted images have on the viewing audience? What purpose is served by depicting criminals and law enforcers in such unrealistic terms? The new breed of "reality-oriented" programs, no matter how far removed from the truth, seeks to give the viewer the impression that "this is how the world really works."

Unfortunately, as social scientists are beginning to discover, people do take cues about behavior and values from what they see on TV. We can only wonder how current television portrayals of criminals and law enforcers are affecting the perceptions of the American public.

Leonard J. Theberge
President
The Media Institute

Executive Summary

For every American who is victimized by crime, several experience crime vicariously each evening on their television sets. But while cops and robbers are a staple of TV entertainment, we know very little about how TV portrays crime and the law. This Media Institute study, directed by Drs. Linda and Robert Lichter, systematically examines the lawbreakers and law enforcers shown during six weeks of television programs aired in 1981.

Major Findings

- **Crime pervades television entertainment.**

  The study identified 250 criminals, almost one per show. They committed 417 crimes, or 1.7 per show.

- **TV crime is far more violent than in real life.**

  Murder is by far the most common crime on television, averaging one killing every two and one-half programs.

  TV crime is over 100 times more likely to involve murder than real life crime.*

  A majority of TV crimes involve violence; TV crime is almost 12 times as likely to be violent as real-life crime.

---

*based on FBI Uniform Crime Reports

- **TV criminals tend to come from the "Establishment."**

  Businessmen are responsible for more crime than any group other than professional criminals. A stock criminal "type" is the wealthy middle-aged businessman motivated by greed.

  Most lawbreakers are middle- or upper-class white males over 30 years old.

- **Most crime is punished; but policemen are rarely the heroes.**

  Almost all TV criminals are caught or thwarted, unlike real life where crime often pays.

  Private eyes and even private citizens are portrayed as much better crime fighters than the police.

  Although a majority of police is shown positively, a substantial minor percentage is either corrupt or incompetent, and heroic cops are rare.

Summary

Television entertainment largely ignores most aspects of real crime in America, focusing instead on the most serious, violent and life-threatening offenses. By sensationalizing crime in this way, TV misses its opportunity to educate the audience about the true dimensions of America's crime problem. FBI statistics show that the public is more likely to confront "street crime" and relatively mundane offenses such as drunkenness, larceny, disorderly conduct and drug abuse. In contrast, murders and violent thefts dominate the world of television crime.

Television's criminals are equally far removed from their real life counterparts. Most crime on TV is committed by either professional criminals or pillars of the community such as well-heeled businessmen and the police themselves. The vast majority of their crime is predicated on pure greed. By focusing on the avarice of the middle and upper classes, television ignores the link between crime and poverty.

In one respect, there is no crime "problem" in the fantasy world of TV entertainment, since most law breakers are inevitably thwarted. Television credits this phenomenal crime busting not to heroic police officers, but to private eyes and private citizens. While police, lawyers and government agents are generally shown as competent upholders of the law, they often need the help of the lone outsider—the private eye or the citizen-detective—to bring evildoers to justice.

Introduction

Crime has become a major concern for most Americans—every year one household in three is touched by crime. In 1979, the National Crime Survey determined that over 40 million people across the United States were victims of attempted criminal offenses. This included over six million people terrorized by illegal activity involving the threat or act of violence.

Nor is there any safe haven from the possibility of being victimized. Crime cuts across the boundaries of age, sex, race, class and geography. Despite the well-documented vulnerability of the elderly to street crime, victimization rates are far higher for young people than for senior citizens. Although women are uniquely victimized by crimes such as rape, males are more likely to be the targets of most violent crimes.

Nonwhites are more vulnerable to crimes of violence than are whites but thieves prey on all racial groups about equally. Poor people are most susceptible to violent crime but the wealthy suffer the highest rate of personal larceny. Finally, while crimes of violence are most prevalent in central cities, suburbanites are just as likely to be plagued by theft. In fact, crimes such as assault, larceny and burglary are more common in small cities than in major metropolises.

Yet for every American unlucky enough to be touched by crime, several experience crime vicariously every evening on their television sets. Cops and robbers, sheriffs and bandits, private eyes and underworld violence have always been staples of television entertainment.

For all the attention that has been lavished on televised violence, however, we know very little about televised crime. Yet crime provides the context for much of the violent and otherwise antisocial behavior that appears on the small screen.

Researchers have found that heavy television watchers perceive the real world as more violent and crime ridden than it actually is. Although the implications of this fact have been disputed, it raises the possibility that televised crime may influence the attitudes and behavior of audiences in ways that are still unknown.[1]

We cannot begin to chart the possible effects of televised crime, however, without first understanding the role it plays in entertainment programs. The purpose of this study is to examine systematically the extent and nature of crime and law enforcement as they are portrayed on prime-time television entertainment. Our approach is to combine the social scientific technique of content analysis with relevant illustrations from the programs themselves. We shall focus first on the types of illegal behavior portrayed and then on the portrayals of those who commit crimes. Finally we examine the other half of the cops and robbers tandem: law enforcers and the nature of law enforcement on television entertainment.

---

[1] Gerbner, George, and Gross, Larry. "Living with Television: The Violence Profile." *Journal of Communication,* 1976, 26, 173–199. For criticism of their findings see Paul Hirsch, "The Scary World of the Nonviewer and Other Anomalies." *Communication Research,* 1980, 7, 403–456; Paul Hirsch, "On Not Learning from One's Own Mistakes." *Communication Research,* 1981, 8, 3–37.

I. Methodology

Using a six-week program sample of prime-time series from the 1980–81 television season, we developed specific categories to code multiple characteristics of each crime committed as well as each criminal and law enforcer portrayed. (Lists of all shows coded are included in Appendices A and B.)

All programs in which at least one crime was committed or a law enforcer appeared were coded. Programs were identified according to series title, broadcast date, network and general program type (comedy vs. adventure/drama).

A criminal was defined as an individual who knowingly or unknowingly violated any local, state or federal criminal statute.

A law enforcer was coded if he was identified as working in an occupation directly related to law enforcement at the local, state or national level, either through information that he or other characters supplied or through the televised work setting.

The content analysis system used for the study took a "conservative" approach, i.e. a character was coded as a criminal or law enforcer only when identified as such in each show. If a character was so defined in one episode but this was not made explicit in another segment he was coded only in the first episode. One could not assume that the television viewer would identify a character as a criminal or law enforcer unless this status was established in each episode. All characters were coded as individuals.

The sex and race of each character were also coded. The latter allowed for all major racial groups likely to be portrayed on television including whites, blacks, Hispanics and those of Oriental extraction. Age was categorized in four major groups: those under 18, those 18 to 30, those aged 30 to 50 and those over 50. While age could not be determined by strict objective criteria, it was possible to fit people into these categories on the basis of their general appearance. (Of course, those on television may seem younger than their actual age.)

The relative economic status of a character was coded when known. These categories included wealthy, middle class and working class or poor.

The continuity of characters was coded according to whether they were major stars of a series, played minor roles on a continuous basis or made only a single appearance. This status was easily established from the show's opening credits which specified these distinctions.

All criminals were classified according to occupation when such information was provided. These categories reflected the nature of criminals' economic endeavors on television rather than any comprehensive listing of actual occupations. These occupational categories included "professional" criminals, their flunkies, police, businessmen, professionals such as doctors and lawyers, blue collar workers and a diverse residual category that included such characters as a carnival announcer and a motorcycle racer.

Each law enforcer was also classified according to his general occupational position. The range of these positions reflected the particular diversity of law-related occupations in television entertainment. Law enforcers fell into six general categories.

First were various types of lawyers, all coded into a single category, since television often failed to specify their particular affiliation. Second were judges at all levels of the judicial system. Third were myriad private investigators. The fourth category contained all police from the "cop on the beat" up the hierarchy to the police commissioner, as well as sheriffs and their deputies. Fifth were other government agents including the FBI, CIA and special investigative personnel from other government agencies such as the Internal Revenue Service who were involved in criminal and law enforcement activities. Finally, a residual category contained law enforcers whose general occupations were not portrayed often enough to justify separate categories. Security guards were classified in this group.

Crimes were coded individually according to definitions provided by the FBI's *Uniform Crime Reports*. Adapting the FBI's latest comprehensive list of crimes[2], we grouped all criminal acts on television into two major categories. *Violent crimes* include murder, robbery, kidnapping, aggravated assault and rape; *serious crimes* include these violent crimes as well as burglary, larceny and motor vehicle theft.

Criminals were also coded according to whether they were first-time or habitual offenders. The motive that propelled each criminal to commit his crime was noted where such information was evident.[3] Among these motives were greed or some other form of self interest, mental imbalance, political, sexual, sympathetic or altruistic motives, personal vendettas, and accidental acts.

The outcome or plot resolution of a character's behavior was coded where known. Possible outcomes included success, failure and various types of character change. Success denoted achieving one's intended goal such as getting away with a crime or capturing the criminal. Defeat occurred when a character did not succeed in his endeavor or was punished for it. A character could also have a change of heart. For example, a criminal could ultimately express genuine regret and declare his intention to turn over a new leaf. In such cases the outcome was coded as repentance.

Finally, the general nature of a law enforcer's plot func-

---

[2] U.S. Department of Justice, Federal Bureau of Investigation. *Uniform Crime Reports: Crime in the United States—1980* (Washington, D.C.: Government Printing Office, 1981). Unless otherwise specified, all references to crime statistics are from this document.

[3] This category was adapted from one used by Joseph R. Dominick in "Crime and Law Enforcement on Prime-Time Television," *Public Opinion Quarterly*, Vol. 37, No. 2, Summer 1973, pp. 241–250.

tion was categorized as positive, negative or neutral. Such judgments were not without an objective basis since television's simplistic plots usually made it easy to distinguish good guys from bad guys. The criteria for these categories can be illustrated by listing the types of negative and positive functions that law enforcers could perform.

Negative functions fell into five categories according to whether a character's behavior was illegal, malevolent, foolish, greedy or incompetent regarding occupational duties. Illegal behavior was defined as those acts which appeared to violate federal, state or local criminal statutes. Malevolent acts were those in which the perpetrator attempted to hurt another person without actually breaking a law. Foolish acts involved behavior held up to ridicule as stupid or socially inappropriate while lacking the directed negative intent of malevolence. Ridicule was indicated either by the reactions of other characters or by audience cues such as canned laughter.

Greedy or self-centered actions were those in which the character tried to maximize his own interests without regard for other people. Although such actions placed others at a disadvantage in some way, the primary motive was to advance one's own interests rather than to hurt someone else purposely.

While some actions appeared to involve more than one negative characteristic, it was possible to define these categories as mutually exclusive. For example, robbing a bank might be seen as foolish and greedy. In this scheme, however, it was coded as illegal since that is the most crucial aspect of this act. The illegality of an act took precedence over any other characteristic.

Other categories were distinguished from each other by the absence or presence of directed negative intent. Trying to prevent someone from obtaining a job he needs because one does not like him personally is an example of malevolence. In this case there is intent to do harm to a specific party. Making a general statement that women are not as smart as men was coded as foolish because there is no negative intent directed at a specific individual.

Becoming obsessed with winning a sports competition while ignoring others' feelings is an example of greed or self-interest (*Enos*—4/15), since the primary motive is to maximize one's gains, not to inflict suffering deliberately on any particular individual. The category of occupational incompetence was coded when the character did not execute his job-related responsibilities rationally and fully, such as failing to investigate thoroughly a suspect's background.

Positive actions could take one of four forms. Actions were coded charitable/philanthropic when some financial resource was given to the less fortunate, usually in the form of a charitable donation. One displayed sympathy or helpful behavior when friendly advice or other nonfinancial assistance was offered to another person. A law enforcer was coded as professionally competent when he attempted to execute responsibly some job-related duty intended to benefit another person or society in general.

The last type of positive action applied to this occupational group was performance beyond the call of duty. This indicated that the law enforcement officer not only pursued his assigned professional tasks but went beyond the scope of those responsibilities in helping others. For example, a lawyer may diligently prepare a defense for his client and also help the client's ailing wife obtain medical assistance.

Those law enforcers who were coded as neutral usually occupied only minor roles and had no discernible positive or negative function within the context of the major plot. An example of a neutral character would be a police officer who asks a fellow officer for advice but does not actually perform any task.

The context within which a law enforcer's behavior occurred was coded as occupational, personal or a combination of the two. An occupational context was coded when the character functioned chiefly in the capacity of a law enforcer, devoid of extraneous personal relations. An example would be a police detective's investigation of a murder.

A personal context was coded when there were no connections with occupational activities. For example, a plot may concern the way a law enforcer deals with his alcoholic teenage son. A combination context was one in which both personal and occupational elements were present. For example, a police officer might investigate a drug ring in which his daughter is involved.

Law enforcers were coded according to whether they "bent" the rules in executing their occupational tasks; this is distinct from violating a criminal statute because it implies violating only an occupational code or rule. For example, in one program a sheriff fails to report to his superiors that his deputies had infiltrated a car theft ring, even though police department rules require him to do so (*Lobo*—3/10).

The outcome or plot resolution of a law enforcer's function was coded where applicable. Outcomes were coded according to the exclusive and direct effects of behavior within the context of the plot. These outcomes included success, failure and various types of character change (or the plot could remain unresolved). Success denoted achieving one's intended goal whether the action was admirable or evil. Examples of success include solving a crime or giving someone advice that helps him in a concrete manner.

Defeat occurred when a character did not succeed in his endeavor or was punished for it. Examples of defeat include going to jail for a crime or being made to look silly for a foolish remark or act. More specifically, those characters involved in solving crimes were coded according to whether they were the primary or secondary agent in solving the crime or whether they were involved but failed to solve the crime themselves.

II. Television's Crime Wave

The 263 programs we reviewed contained a total of 250 criminals who committed 417 crimes. That works out to almost one criminal and 1.7 crimes per show across the entire evening schedule. There can be no question, then, that crime is a prevalent activity on television entertainment shows.

Nine out of ten crimes occurred on dramas like *CHiPs* and *Dynasty*, although that genre accounted for only a minority of the programs viewed. The prevalence of comedy shows during prime time is accounted for partly by audience taste and partly by scheduling constraints. Many more sitcoms than dramas fit snugly into 30-minute time slots. So there are more comedies scheduled, although proportionately more time per program is given over to dramas.

Some crimes did occur on situation comedies, such as a *Barney Miller* episode where an irrate restaurant customer assaults a waiter who demeaned his looks (3/12). Most crimes, however, were committed on adventure series. These included programs like an episode of *The Greatest American Hero* where a business executive who manufactures "classified" equipment for the government commits treason by selling secrets to an enemy country (4/15), as well as cops and robbers shows like *Hill Street Blues* which features a variety of crimes ranging from common pickpockets (4/4) to a rapist who stalks his victims in a local park (3/28).

Just as striking as the sheer number of crimes are the types of crime portrayed. Television scripts rarely deal with the mundane and humdrum activities that occupy the cop on the beat. Real policemen spend much of their time dealing with such "low-profile" crimes as drunkenness, disorderly conduct, breaking and entering and vandalism. By contrast, their television counterparts are confronted with an overwhelming tide of murders, muggings and assaults.

In short, the bulk of crime on television is far more serious than in real life. It consists largely of vicious attacks by calculating criminals on innocent victims. This is shown graphically by Table 1, which enumerates the various types of crimes portrayed on television. Murder, the most serious crime of all, is also by far the most common crime on television. Our study recorded over 100 murders, or roughly one homicide every two and one half programs.

The ingenuity of scriptwriters never seems to flag when it comes to concocting settings for homicides. Thus, a psycho-

Table 1. Crimes Portrayed on TV Entertainment Programs.

Crime	Frequency	Percent
Murder	101	24
Robbery	65	16
Kidnapping	37	9
Aggravated Assault	35	8
Bribery	19	5
Burglary	18	4
Drug-Related	17	4
Blackmail	14	3
Fraud	14	3
Gambling	12	3
Larceny (theft)	10	2
Extortion	7	2
Rape	7	2
Embezzlement	6	2
Auto Theft	5	1
Vandalism	5	1
Liquor Offenses	4	1
Loan Sharking	4	1
Other	37	9
	417	100%

Note: Percentages in tables may not sum to 100 percent because of rounding.

pathic hairdresser on the now-defunct *Vegas* murders several of his female customers (3/4). On *Hart to Hart,* a ship's captain, who uses his pleasure cruises to distribute counterfeit money to unsuspecting passengers, similarly disposes of a private investigator who infiltrates his operation (4/14).

Overall, such murders accounted for almost one crime in four shown on prime-time television. The preponderance of homicides sets the tone for television's portrayal of illegal activity. All the commonly depicted crimes involved the threat or use of force against other people. In addition to murder, these crimes included robbery, kidnapping and aggravated assault. Together these four categories of crime added up to 57 percent of all those coded. No other single category made up as much as 5 percent of the total.

After murder, robbery was the most prevalent form of unlawful behavior, accounting for almost one crime in six. For example, a team of muggers accosts the elderly on an episode of *Mork and Mindy* (4/16), while an armed teenager holds up a grocery store on *Hill Street Blues* (3/28). Robbery, as defined in the FBI Uniform Crime Reports, always involves force or the threat of force. This reliance on actual or threatened violence distinguishes robbery from simple larceny (theft) and burglary.

The other two most common offenses during prime time, kidnapping and aggravated assault, each accounted for about one crime in 12. The former was illustrated by a *Fantasy Island* segment on which a young man kidnaps his own girlfriend to extort money from her wealthy father (4/18). The latter is exemplified by a *Dynasty* script that calls for a hired thug to administer a brutal beating to an adversary of series star Blake Carrington (3/9). Just as robbery is a more serious and violent crime than simple theft, aggravated assault is quite different from a simple fistfight or shoving match. It consists of an attack aimed at inflicting severe injury, often involving the use of a weapon. Simple assault, by contrast, involves neither a weapon nor serious injury.

In sum, the majority of crimes shown on prime-time television were quite serious, involving personal attacks that carried at least the potential for serious injury or death. Of course, many other crimes were portrayed, some more serious than others. Nine additional categories each comprised between 2 and 5 percent of all instances of televised crime. In descending order of frequency these categories included bribery, burglary (breaking and entering), drug-related offenses, blackmail, fraud, gambling, larceny or theft, extortion and rape. Combining these with the "big four" of murder, robbery, kidnapping and aggravated assault results in 13 categories that account for 86 percent of all televised crime.

By contrast, such everyday "garden variety" crimes as prostitution, drunk driving, receiving stolen property, minor sex offenses and weapons offenses each accounted for less than one half of 1 percent of all prime-time crime.

Crime: TV vs. Reality

Relatively few types of crime (and the more serious crimes at that) account for most of the illegal activities television uses to entertain its prime-time audience. To indicate the extent to which this behavior is weighted toward the most violent and dangerous crimes we can compare these findings with FBI data on actual crime in America.

Direct comparisons are not easy to come by since most FBI statistics are based on arrest records, rather than reports of crime. Unlike much real-life crime, however, televised crime usually leads to arrest; the figures are roughly comparable in this regard.

The relative frequency of real life crimes is indicated by Table 2. It suggests that, after an evening spent watching television, a trip to the precinct house might be something of a letdown. At the top of the FBI's list are drunk driving, larceny (theft without violence), drunkenness, disorderly conduct and drug abuse, which together account for a majority of all arrests nationwide. Compared to TV's concentration on murder, robbery, kidnapping and aggravated assault these transgressions seem positively prosaic. In descending order of frequency, the drunk and disorderly, thieves and drug abusers are followed by such relatively

Table 2. Total Arrests, All Crimes 1980 FBI Statistics. (%)

Drunk Driving	14
Larceny	12
Drunkenness	11
Disorderly Conduct	8
Drug Abuse	6
Burglary	5
Simple Assault	5
Fraud	3
Aggravated Assault	3
Vandalism	2
Weapons Offenses	2
Runaways	2
Robbery	1
Motor Vehicle Thefts	1
Rape	*
Murder	*
Kidnapping	*
Other	25
Total	100%

*Less than 1 percent

Source: *Crime in America 1980*, compiled by the FBI and published by the Government Printing Office. Unless otherwise noted, this is the source of all FBI crime statistics cited in this report.

minor malefactors as those charged with burglary, simple assault and fraud.

The first of TV's high-visibility crimes to appear on the list is aggravated assault. It ranks ninth, accounting for only 3 percent of all arrests. Even so, serious assaults are far more common than robberies. Forcible thefts comprise only 1 percent of all arrests in real life, compared to one in every six crimes on television. Yet even robberies are far more common than murders, which dominate crime on the airwaves. In 1980 only one-fifth of 1 percent of all arrests were for murder or non-negligent manslaughter. As a proportion of all crimes, therefore, murders are over 100 times more frequent on television than in real life. As for kidnappings, they occur so infrequently that the FBI does not bother to list them as a separate category.

Of course, a policeman's life may not be dull, but neither

is it always entertaining to others. One could hardly expect many television plots to revolve around cases of vandalism and littering. And while drunkenness may be a major health problem, how many ways can you film *The Days of Wine and Roses?* Nine hours of nightly prime time quickly consumes an awesome amount of plotting and dialogue, and it's easier to maintain audience interest with dastardly deeds than with the relatively humdrum stuff of everyday police work. Over the long run, *Dragnet's* Joe Friday just can't compete with James Bond.

And yet, given the need to entertain and titillate an audience increasingly jaded by the whirl of modern life, television's fantasy world remains a surprisingly dangerous place. Even when we restrict our attention to the most serious crimes, television selects out the darkest and most violent side of human behavior for its stories.

To demonstrate this, we need only examine the relative incidence of the most serious categories of crime in real life. Serious crimes are those which comprise the FBI Crime Index, which serves as the basis for most of the FBI's yearly reports on the crime rate. Included in the Crime Index are murder and nonnegligent manslaughter, forcible rape, robbery, aggravated assault, burglary, larceny and motor vehicle theft.

In 1980 these serious crimes accounted for 23 percent of all arrests excluding minor traffic offenses. In the programs we viewed from the 1980–81 television season the same offenses accounted for a majority (57 percent) of the crimes portrayed. With the addition of kidnappings, which are too infrequent to even appear on the FBI's list, serious crimes make up 66.7 percent or precisely two-thirds of all prime-time crime. Even more striking is the discrepancy between the relative proportion of violent crime on television and in real life. Violent crimes (murder, rape, aggravated assault, robbery and kidnapping) accounted for only 5 percent of all arrests in 1980; on television they accounted for 59 percent of illegal acts. So televised crime was almost 12 times as likely to be violent as was real-life crime, as measured by arrests during roughly the same time period.

The ultimate violent crime, murder, ran through a variety of series. A stockbroker on *Vegas* who "owns" a high-class call girl ring kills two of his employees because they want out of the operation (4/1). On *Walking Tall* an industrialist orders the murder of an employee who discovers that he has been illegally dumping toxic wastes (3/24). And on *The Greatest American Hero* right-wing terrorists kill an FBI agent who investigates their plot to seize control of the country (3/18).

The more mundane but pervasive real-life crimes are largely neglected. In fact, drunk driving was portrayed on only one program in our sample, an episode of *CHiPs* (4/19). According to National Highway Traffic Safety Administration estimates, alcohol is implicated in as many as half the traffic fatalities each year.[4] That means that mixing driving and drink is responsible for more deaths each year than the total number of homicides—yet on television, murders are portrayed about 100 times as often as drunk driving.

To fine tune these comparisons, we can examine the frequency of each major offense as a proportion of all serious crimes on television and in reality. An advantage of this procedure is that the FBI publishes totals of all reported offenses (not simply arrests) for serious crime only.

Table 3 reveals the very different proportions of major crimes that appear on television and in real life. It shows that most serious crime is directed toward property rather than people and does not involve the use or threat of force. On the 1980 FBI Crime Index, almost nine out of ten offenses are burglaries or thefts that involve no physical danger for the victim. Only one serious crime in ten involves violence. Murder, rape and kidnapping each account for less than 1 percent of all serious crimes. Aggravated assault and robbery, i.e. theft involving force or its threat, each account for only about one serious crime in 20.

On television, the proportions of crime against people and property are almost exactly reversed. Crimes of violence make up seven out of eight serious offenses, while

---

[4] U.S. Department of Transportation, National Highway Traffic Safety Administration. *Fatal Accident Reporting System 1980* (Washington, D.C.: Government Printing Office).

Table 3. Serious Crimes on 1981 TV Entertainment Programs Compared to 1980 Reports. (%)

	TV	FBI
Murder	36	*
Rape	3	*
Kidnapping	13	*
Aggravated Assault	13	5
Robbery	23	4
Burglary	6	28
Larceny-Theft	6	62
Total	100%	100%
Violent Crime	88	10
Property Crime	12	90
Total	100%	100%

*Less than 1 percent
Note: Figures are percentages of all FBI Crime Index listings; larceny category includes motor vehicle theft.

theft and burglary together account for only one crime in eight.

The audience does witness a few crimes of the sort that usually occupy law enforcers, such as a simple purse snatching on *Hill Street Blues* (4/21). However, they are far more likely to be treated to such fare as a *Magnum, P.I.* episode in which a man kills his girlfriend when she tries to leave him (4/2), or a *Flamingo Road* segment in which a woman tries to murder her own sister to resolve a romantic triangle (4/2).

The differences between fantasy and life are sharpest at opposite ends of the Crime Index spectrum. Simple thefts alone account for nearly two-thirds of the FBI Crime Index but only 6 percent of serious crimes on television. At the other extreme, murders alone make up over one-third of all serious crimes on television but only a miniscule one-sixth of 1 percent of the FBI Crime Index figures. Thus, even after all but the most serious crimes are excluded from the comparison, prime-time crime is over 200 times more likely to involve homicide than is real-life crime.

In summary, crime on television is more dangerous, more

violent and more likely to be directed against persons than is actual crime. The latest FBI statistics indicate that the most common offenses are rarely seen on television, while the most brutal and injurious crimes appear far out of proportion to their occurrence in everyday life.

III. Criminals In TV Entertainment

Television's portrayal of criminals also diverges markedly from real life. According to the latest FBI arrest reports, crimes are disproportionately committed by males, young people, nonwhites, the poor and the unemployed. They act out of a wide variety of motives, and more often than not their crimes go unpunished.

In the fantasy world of prime-time television most of these relationships are reversed. The bulk of prime-time criminals are male but they also tend to be white middle- or upper-class adults. Their transgressions usually stem directly from simple greed and they are usually thwarted before the closing credits. We shall consider each of these characteristics of TV criminals in turn.

Sex

Most crimes in America are committed by males, and television accurately reflects the disproportionate tendency of men to commit illegal acts. As Table 4 shows, males accounted for 84 percent of all arrests in 1980, including 90 percent of arrests for violent crimes. The proportions on television are about the same. About nine of ten criminals were males regardless of the severity of the offense. Male criminals ranged from a purse snatcher on *Hill Street Blues* (4/21) to a male involved in a drug-related murder on *Hart to Hart* (3/3).

Table 4. Crime Rate by Sex. Comparison of TV Entertainment
and FBI Arrest Reports. (%)

Sex	All Crime		Violent Crime	
	TV	FBI	TV	FBI
Male	89	84	90	90
Female	11	16	10	10
	100%	100%	100%	100%

Age

Youthful offenders have been much in the news of late. Especially disturbing is the rise in serious and violent crimes among teenagers. In 1980, young people not yet 18 years old accounted for over one arrest in five across the country. Even more ominous, these teenagers and subteens made up 36 percent of those arrested for FBI Index crimes—serious offenses ranging from robbery and larceny to rape and murders. More broadly, young people (mostly young males) are implicated in the vast majority of crimes in the United States. The 18 to 29 year-old age group alone accounted for virtually half of all arrests in 1980. Overall, people not yet 30 years old totalled 70 percent of all recorded arrests for that year.

Arrest records for serious crimes are skewed even more heavily toward young offenders. The under-30s group made up 82 percent of those arrested for offenses that comprise the FBI Crime Index. Finally, individuals still in their teens or 20s made up nearly three out of four arrests for crimes of violence.

On television, as Table 5 shows, the relationship between youth and criminality was reversed. The vast majority of criminals were mature adults over age 30. This held true for both violent and non-violent crimes, as well as for both serious and minor offenses. A majority of criminals was found in the 30 to 50 age group, including 59 percent of those responsible for both serious and violent crime. Another one in five criminals was over age 50, as was one in six violent

Table 5. Crime Rate by Age Group.
Comparison of TV Entertainment and FBI Arrest Reports. (%)

AGE	All Crime		Serious Crime		Violent Crime	
	TV	FBI	TV	FBI	TV	FBI
Under 18	6	21	7	36	8	19
18–30	18	49	18	46	18	55
30–50	57	23	59	15	59	23
Over 50	19	7	16	3	15	3
	100%	100%	100%	100%	100%	100%

criminals. By contrast, only about one criminal in four was under 30, regardless of the seriousness of the offense.

In real life a majority of those arrested for violent crimes is between the ages of 18 and 30. In the shows we viewed only 18 percent of the criminal characters came from this age group. Equally striking is the near absence of youth crime on television. Characters not yet 18 years old accounted for only 6 percent of all criminals, 7 percent of those who commit serious crimes and 8 percent of those guilty of illegal acts of violence.

Not a single teenager under 18 committed a murder on the 263 shows we watched although this age group accounted for 1,742 murder arrests in 1980 or almost one homicide arrest in ten nationwide. Rather, the norm on television was represented by a middle-aged real estate manager involved in land swindles (*BJ and the Bear*—3/10), and a drug dealer of similar age who finds murder necessary to keep his business going (*Hart to Hart*—3/3).

There are few crimes by television teens such as the involvement of three teenagers in a car theft ring on *CHiPs* (9/13). More common are crimes by those over 50 such as an aging police sergeant on *Enos* (4/15) who pushes heroin on the side, and an ambitious politician on *The Greatest American Hero* who is involved in both murder and an attempted assassination of the President (3/18).

In sum, youth crime is a major concern for both law enforcers and the general public. In the fantasy world of television, however, it is hardly ever a problem. Instead crime is largely the province of mature adults.

Race

In 1980, 25 percent of those arrested in America for crimes were black, another 2 percent were Asian or American Indian and the remaining 74 percent were white. Blacks accounted for 33 percent of those arrested for serious crimes, other nonwhites 2 percent and whites 65 percent. Arrestees for violent crimes were 44 percent black, 1 percent other nonwhite and 54 percent white.

So blacks are arrested about twice as often as one would expect on the basis of their distribution in the population. For serious crimes this factor rises to nearly three to one, and for crimes of violence almost four to one. Similar results can be obtained from FBI victimization statistics (victims' reports of suspects' characteristics),[5] making it unlikely that these arrest totals are greatly inflated by racism on the part of the arresting officers.

It should be noted, of course, that blacks are disproportionately represented among the victims as well as the perpetrators of crimes. As Lee Daniels recently wrote in the *New York Times Magazine,* "because the poor are more victimized by crime than others, blacks, who represent a disproportionate percentage of the poor, are more likely than whites to be the victims of violent crimes." Daniels also points out that blacks are particularly vulnerable to street crime, and "the primary reason for most 'black on black' crime ... is that most street crimes are committed by poor people out of desperation, impulse and opportunity."[6] Beyond this we lack the competence to enter the debate over the societal causes for this differential crime rate. Our far more limited purpose is to compare these figures with comparable data from prime-time television.

---

[5] U.S. Department of Justice, Bureau of Justice Statistics. *Criminal Victimization in the United States, 1979* (Washington, D.C.: Government Printing Office, 1981).

[6] Lee Daniels, "Black Crime, Black Victims," *New York Times Magazine,* May 16, 1982, pp. 39–44.

Table 6. Crime Rate by Race.
Comparison of TV Entertainment and FBI Arrest Reports. (%)

	All Crime		Serious Crime		Violent Crime	
Race	TV	FBI	TV	FBI	TV	FBI
White	88	74	88	65	90	54
Nonwhite	12	26	12	35	10	46
	100%	100%	100%	100%	100%	100%

Studies have shown that by the late 1960s black characters were written into television programs roughly in proportion to their distribution in the actual population, i.e., 10 to 12 percent of all characters. We found that they make up about the same proportion of criminals on prime-time shows. As Table 6 indicates, nonwhite characters, almost all of them black, accounted for 12 percent of all criminals on the shows we viewed. The proportion dropped to 10 percent of perpetrators of violent crime and only 3 percent of the murderers. Illustrative of the relatively few black criminals is a drug dealer on *Barney Miller* (4/16) and a hotel maid who stole the tips of other maids on *The Jeffersons* (3/19).

What are we to make of this disparity? We would hardly recommend that television scriptwriters assign more murders to black characters for the dubious purpose of bringing television closer to "reality". But the very absurdity of such a suggestion raises an important point about the social content of television entertainment. It is very difficult to interpret the relative paucity of televised crime (especially violent crime) among blacks as simply a reflection of reality. Instead these figures may reflect concerns of television writers, producers and network executives to avoid reinforcing negative stereotypes and producing negative role models. Whether such concerns are conscious or unconscious, individual or institutional, they illustrate the point that television entertainment does convey social values.

Nor is there necessarily anything invidious about this fact. It was partly criticism from the black community, after all, that led to the disappearance of "Stepin Fetchit" characters

Table 7. Crime Rate by Occupation on TV Entertainment Programs. (%)

	All Crime	Homicide
Gangsters*	36	31
Businessmen*	24	26
Police	13	6
Professionals	8	11
Blue Collar	5	5
Other Flunkies	5	11
Other	9	10
	100%	100%

*Includes flunkies who were ordered to commit crimes by bosses in these occupational categories.

in popular entertainment and made possible a series like *Roots*. Whether or not the relatively low violent crime rate among black characters reflects conscious concerns of this sort, it suggests that the creators of TV entertainment cannot ignore their role in communicating images laden with social values.

Occupation

Most criminals in television belong to relatively few occupational groups. Of those whose occupation was identified, over three out of four criminals fit into one of four categories: professional criminals, businessmen, police and flunkies who do the dirty work for someone else.

Table 7 presents the occupational profile of prime-time criminals. First and foremost were people whose only profession is crime itself. This group included members of organized crime as well as independent gangs of thieves. Twenty-eight percent of all prime-time criminals were people whose entire income derived from the proceeds of their evildoing. The addition of their flunkies raises this group's total to 36 percent or more than one prime-time criminal in three. So TV pictures a world inhabited by legions of full-time criminals who earn their livelihoods at the expense of law-abiding citizens.

These groups of "professional" deviants are illustrated by a drug smuggler on *BJ and the Bear* (3/24) and a gang leader on *CHiPs* who reaps the profits from a widespread car theft ring (9/13). Typical of the flunkies or underlings of professional crime is a thug hired by *Dynasty's* Blake Carrington to beat up his daughter's suitor (3/9).

Yet by no means is most TV crime the product of social deviants or criminal subcultures. Instead it can be traced to established figures in the social order such as well-off professionals, policemen and, above all, businessmen. About one criminal in eight was identified as a businessman. As we found with professional criminals, however, this group became considerably larger when their flunkies were taken into account. Businessmen and their flunkies together accounted for 24 percent of all criminals with identifiable occupations, far exceeding any other legitimate occupational group.

For example, the owner of a computer firm and his flunky are involved in shipping illegal explosives for profit (*BJ and the Bear*—4/14). Similarly, a theater owner on *Lobo* (3/3) and his ruthless underling not only embezzle company funds but commit a murder to cover up the theft (3/3). We have already noted the business executive who tries to sell "classified" equipment to an enemy country (*The Greatest American Hero*—4/15) and how *Dynasty* executive Blake Carrington has his adversaries beaten up by hired thugs (3/9). Other examples include a stockbroker who murders his call girls (*Vegas*—4/1); a casino owner who skims the profits (*Vegas*—4/15); the owner of a chemical company who falsifies records and attempts murder to cover up his illegal dumping of toxic substances (*Walking Tall*—3/24); the head of a world-wide conglomerate who kills a competitor (*Nero Wolfe*—3/27); a bank manager who arranges to have his own bank robbed (*Lobo*—4/7); the owner of a record company who steals recordings from other companies (*Lobo*—4/21); a theater owner who embezzles company funds (*Lobo*—3/3); the owner of a dating service who blackmails employees (*BJ and the Bear*—4/7); and the head of a real estate company who organizes land swindles (*BJ and the Bear*—3/10).

Crooks, Conmen and Clowns, a Media Institute study of businessmen in TV entertainment, found that a high proportion of business characters are portrayed as criminals.[7] We now find that the converse is true as well; a substantial segment of TV's criminal population is drawn from the world of business.

Police officers came next in the line-up of offenders. On television the upholders of law and order made up 13 percent of those who broke the law, about one criminal in eight. Included here were a police officer on *Magnum, P.I.* who accepts a bribe to look the other way during a traffic violation (4/23) and a police lieutenant on *The Greatest American Hero* (9/3) who attempts to steal some "hot" diamonds from the original thieves.

They were followed by professional people such as doctors, lawyers and architects who together accounted for 8 percent of all criminals. Typical of them was a doctor on *Hart to Hart* who runs a counterfeiting ring (4/14) and a lawyer on *Vegas* who draws his profits from pornography (3/25).

The occupational group least likely to contain lawbreakers consisted of blue collar workers, who comprised only 5 percent of all criminals whose occupations were known. Among the few blue collar criminals was a gardener on *Magnum, P.I.* who pilfers already stolen money from a gang of criminals (4/16).

The remainder was scattered among such characters as a model who murders her husband to collect money he had already stolen (*Hart to Hart*—3/10) and a carnival announcer who runs fixed gambling games (*BJ and the Bear*—4/7).

In sum, of criminals with known occupations, over one-third were professional criminals or their flunkies, another one-fourth were businessmen and their underlings, one in eight were policemen, one in 12 came from the educated professions and only one in 20 held blue collar jobs. So television focuses far more on criminals near the top of the

---

[7] Leonard Theberge, ed., *Crooks, Conmen and Clowns: Businessmen in TV Entertainment* (Washington, D.C.: The Media Institute, 1981).

Table 8. Crime Rate by Economic Status
on TV Entertainment Programs. (%)

Status	All Crimes	Homicides
Poor	3	0
Middle Class	4	8
Wealthy	16	20
Unknown	77	72
	100%	100%

social hierarchy than on those whose activities stem from a culture of poverty. The Hollywood gangster of 1930s films, who turned to a life of crime to escape the hopelessness of Hell's Kitchen, has no equivalent on television today. Even the professional criminals are usually members of lucrative organizations, and most other lawbreakers are either pillars of the community or those sworn to protect it.

Economic Status

The image of evil-doing in high places is reinforced by the economic status accorded characters who commit crimes. To be sure, the status of most characters could not be clearly identified. Only one in four could be reliably coded as either rich, middle class or poor. However, that left 58 criminals with a clear place in the economic hierarchy. And this group was strongly weighted toward the top as Table 8 demonstrates. Sixteen percent of all criminals were clearly wealthy, compared to only 4 percent who were middle class and 3 percent who were poor or working class. Thus, a viewer was about five times more likely to see a wealthy criminal than a poor one. Moreover, the number of wealthy criminals was more than double that of middle- and lower-class criminals combined.

Typical of wealthy criminals is the notorious Boss Hogg of *The Dukes of Hazzard* who uses blackmail to obtain a piece of valuable art (3/13). The even richer and equally notorious Blake Carrington of *Dynasty*, who inhabits a luxurious mansion, knowingly allows company funds to be used illegally (3/9). Among the middle-class offenders is a medical exam-

examiner on *Quincy* who is an accessory in covering up a murder (4/8). Among the few poor characters is a ghetto youth on *Hill Street Blues* who tries to hold up a grocery store (4/21).

The data for homicides are even more striking. Eighty percent of the murders were committed by characters with no clear economic status, 20 percent by wealthy characters and none by either middle-class or poor characters. So among those characters whose economic status was known, murder was the exclusive province of the rich. In real life, of course, crime is associated with low social and economic status. According to Department of Justice Statistics, one-third of the inmates in state prisons were unemployed in the month prior to their arrest. Among those who had income from any source, the average income was almost 50 percent lower than that of comparable groups in the general population.[8]

How much crime is directly and indirectly caused by poverty is a matter of interpretation. But no one would dispute that crime is associated with poverty and unemployment. Yet the TV watcher rarely sees this kind of crime. Instead the viewer is primarily exposed to stories about well-to-do criminals or those without a clearly defined economic status.

Recidivism

In addition to establishing a demographic profile of prime-time criminals, we were interested in determining the number of recidivists, or repeat offenders. Television portrays two types of lawbreakers—the first offender and the habitual criminal. There seems to be no middle ground; a character either commits a crime for the very first time or he is committed to a life of crime. As might be expected from the high proportion of professional criminals, most fell into the latter category.

As Table 9 shows, habitual criminals outnumbered first

---

[8] In addition to *Uniform Crime Reports*, op.cit., see U.S. Department of Justice, Law Enforcement Assistance Administration, *Myths and Realities About Crime* (Washington, D.C.: Government Printing Office, 1981).

**Table 9. Crime Rate by Recidivism
on TV Entertainment Programs. (%)**

First Offender	10
Habitual Criminal	46
Unknown	44
	100%

offenders by more than a four-to-one margin. In 44 percent of the cases the plot didn't make clear whether the bad guy was a first timer or a repeater. Another 46 percent, almost half of all criminals, were clearly identified as recidivists. Only 10 percent were shown committing their first illegal act. For example, *Fantasy Island* featured a young woman whose crime debut involves aiding her boyfriend in an extortion scheme against her own father (4/18). Many more, however, were repeat offenders such as a mobster on *Magnum, P.I.* who, upon his release from prison, engages in robbery and murder to obtain already stolen money (4/23). Another recent parolee on *Hart to Hart* kidnaps the show's heroine for a fat ransom from her wealthy husband (4/21).

The high proportion of recidivists relative to first offenders suggests that prime-time criminals are rarely portrayed as the victims of ill luck or transient emotion. More often they habitually violate the law, often in pursuit of a criminal lifestyle.

Many of the crimes in real life are committed by repeat offenders. An FBI study found that, of over 250,000 people arrested for serious crimes during the period 1970–1975, 64 percent had been arrested at least once before.[9] These repeat offenders had been arrested an average of four times each over a period of five years. But even if we were to consider all repeat offenders as career criminals, which is clearly not the case, their incidence would not equal the picture presented on television. Among the prime-time characters who were specifically identified as either first

---

[9] U.S. Department of Justice, Federal Bureau of Investigation. *Uniform Crime Reports: Crime in America—1976* (Washington, D.C.: Government Printing Office, 1977).

Table 10. *Crime Rate by Motive
on TV Entertainment Programs. (%)*

Motive	All Crimes	Homicides
Greed	74	75
Personal Vendetta	6	9
Mental Imbalance	3	1
Political	2	1
Sexual	6	6
Sympathetic	4	2
Accidental	1	2
Unexplained	4	4
	100%	100%

offenders or habitual criminals, 82 percent fell into the latter group.

Motive

So far we have concentrated on who commits crimes in television entertainment. We turn now to the question of why crimes are carried out. In real life motives for crimes are often murky, mysterious or multiple. Often the perpetrator himself can't sort out the tangled strands of motivation that lead him to break the law.

On television entertainment, however, one motive stands head and shoulders above all others in accounting for crimes of almost every sort. That motive is greed. On television, as Table 10 indicates, greed alone was the motivation of three out of four criminals or 74 percent overall including large majorities of every crime category except rape. Every single embezzler and drug dealer was motivated by greed, along with at least four out of five gamblers, blackmailers, extortionists, bribers, robbers and thieves. This greed was often calculated and cruel, as with a young man who robs a bank on *Lobo* and takes some of its customers hostage (4/7), and a dogbreeder on *Nero Wolfe* who feigns concern for his cousin then carefully plots her murder to inherit her money (3/6).

Other motives occasionally surfaced, although no additional category explained the behavior of more than a small proportion of the 250 criminal characters. Fifteen criminals were carrying on personal vendettas, such as a gangster on *Hill Street Blues* who assaults an opposing gang member specifically to stir up trouble for series hero Captain Frank Furillo (4/4).

Another 14 acted out of some sexual motivation including all seven rapists. Each of these categories accounted for only about 6 percent of all criminals. Another 4 percent had sympathetic motives such as a computer operator who, on pain of losing his job (and with a pregnant wife to support), reluctantly falsifies a report to the EPA hiding the fact that his boss is illegally disposing toxic wastes (*Walking Tall*— 3/24).

Only 3 percent were insane or mentally imbalanced such as a disturbed Vietnam veteran on *CHiPs* who vandalizes small farm pesticide sprayers because he had been a pilot releasing defoliation chemicals in Vietnam. He is turned over to a veterans hospital for treatment (4/5).

One percent, or three characters, broke the law by accident. The motives of the remaining 4 percent were not made clear by the plot. All these categories were obviously dwarfed by the 184 criminals who acted on the basis of avarice. Precise comparisons with the motivations of actual criminals are mostly unavailable. However, the FBI does publish statistics on the motives and circumstances surrounding homicides. Although their categories differ from ours, they provide some indication of the different motivations of murderers in real life and in TV entertainment.

On television the motives of murderers were not very different from those of other criminals. An overwhelming majority, 75 percent, killed because of greed. Nine percent dispatched their victims as the denouement of a personal vendetta. Six percent of the killers had some sexual motive. The motives of 4 percent were never explained. That left only 6 percent who killed for any other reason.

This breakdown can be compared to the FBI's 1980 statistics summarized in Table 11. They show that by far the

Table 11. Murder Circumstances/Motives, 1980 FBI Statistics. (%)

Felony Total	*17.7*
Robbery	10.8
Narcotics	1.7
Sex Offenses	1.5
Other Felony	3.7
Suspected Felony	*6.7*
Argument Total	*44.7*
Romantic Triangle	2.3
Influence of Alcohol/Narcotics	4.8
Property or Money	2.6
Other Arguments	35.0
Other Motives Or Circumstances	*15.9*
Unknown	*15.9*
	100%

largest number of murders—almost half—were committed in the course of arguments (the so-called "crimes of passion" rather than crimes of greed). Another one in four were proven or suspected to result from some other felonious activity such as robbery, rape, etc. Fifteen percent of homicides were of unknown motivation and a slightly larger proportion were brought together under the catch-all category of "other motives."

From this entire list only about one in seven murders could be taken at face value as the product of greed. That represents the combination of 11 percent of murders attributable to robberies and a scant 3 percent that resulted from arguments over property or money. Although greed may be a hidden element standing behind many of the other categories, it is clearly not the major cause of most homicides as it is on television.

On prime time, then, criminals rarely act out of monetary passion, mental imbalance, political conviction or any of the other myriad causes that lead people to break the law. In television entertainment the lawbreaker usually wants just one thing—he wants more.

Table 12. Crime Rate by Plot Resolution on TV Entertainment Programs. (%)

	All Crimes	Serious Crimes	Violent Crimes
Success	8	5	4
Defeat	68	79	80
Character Change	4	4	4
Unresolved	20	12	12
	100%	100%	100%

Resolution

Criminals on television are a bad lot. Most are the perpetrators of particularly brutish acts which they consciously choose to commit on the basis of pure self-interest. Viewers will be relieved to learn, however, that most get their just desert before the final credits.

As Table 12 shows, over two out of three criminals in our sample were defeated—either arrested, killed or otherwise thwarted in their aims. Compared to the 68 percent who suffered defeat, success was achieved by a miniscule 8 percent, or one criminal in 12. Another 4 percent resolved to change their ways and the remaining 20 percent came to no clear plot resolution. A common fate for criminals was exemplified by a drug-dealing police sergeant on *Enos* who is captured by his own men (4/15), and an extortionist on *Vegas* who is killed by his even greedier partner (3/25).

If these results are reassuring to law and order advocates, the comparable figures for serious crimes provide even greater relief. About four out of five TV lawbreakers who committed FBI Index crimes were defeated and only 5 percent were successful. The figures for homicide were virtually identical: 81 percent defeated, only 5 percent successful and 14 percent unresolved.

Anyone faintly familiar with the criminal justice system is aware that these figures bear little relation to the realities of crime and punishment in America. The most recent FBI Crime Index figures indicate that, in the majority of cases, crime does pay. Table 13 shows that of all serious crimes in 1980, fewer than one in five resulted in an arrest. Moreover,

Table 13. Crimes Cleared by Arrest, 1980 FBI Statistics. (%)

	Serious Crimes	Violent Crimes
Arrest	19	44
No Arrest	81	56
	100%	100%

this "clearance" rate of 19 percent for Index crimes does not take into account whether the actual perpetrator was the one arrested or whether the arrest ultimately led to conviction. The police did somewhat better in the case of violent crimes, achieving a clearance rate of 44 percent. Yet even that arrest rate means that a substantial majority of violent crimes went unsolved.

On television, by contrast, even combining the successful perpetrators of serious crimes with those whose fates were not resolved produced only one in six who escaped punishment. The results for violent criminals were virtually identical. Of course it is hardly surprising that TV scripts punish the perpetrators of violent and evil deeds. We note only that the self-imposed principle that crime must not pay during prime time brings the scriptwriters into conflict with real life.

IV. Law Enforcers—A Profile

A total of 373 law enforcers appeared in the programs we viewed. Law enforcers could be seen regularly on the three networks in both comedies and dramas. Slightly over half of all law enforcers (54 percent) appeared on NBC, 27 percent on ABC and the remaining 19 percent on CBS. An over-whelming majority, 81 percent, appeared on adventures or dramas such as *Magnum, P.I.* and *Hill Street Blues* while 19 percent were on comedies such as *Barney Miller* and *Three's Company.*

These guardians of justice were not solely confined to typical cops and robbers shows. Thirty-five percent appeared on series whose major characters were not police or private eyes. Law enforcers were spread about evenly among the three major types of characters. Thirty percent were series stars such as police captain Frank Furillo of *Hill Street Blues,* and private eye Thomas Magnum from the show of the same name. Minor continuing characters, such as the police chief on *Lobo,* constituted 41 percent of the sample. Finally, 29 percent made only a single appearance. Such characters included a district attorney on *Nero Wolfe* and a police sergeant on *The Greatest American Hero.*

Television's protectors of law and order comprised a varied collection of occupational groups as Table 14 shows. The single largest group (71 percent) was represented by various ranks of police, from the captain on *Enos* to the patrol officers of *CHiPs.* Lawyers such as public defender Joyce Davenport of *Hill Street Blues* made up 17 percent of

Table 14. *Prime-Time Television Characters*
with Law Enforcement Occupations. (%)

Police	*71*
Patrolman	14
Sergeant	8
Lieutenant	7
Captain	6
Detective	9
Chief	3
Deputy Sheriff	8
Sheriff	7
Other	9
Lawyers	*16*
Private Practice	2
Public Interest	2
District Attorney	3
Judge	2
Other	7
Private Investigators	*8*
Government Agents	*4*
Other	*1*
Total	100%
Number of Cases	373

the sample. Seven percent were private investigators such as the title character of *Nero Wolfe.* Four percent of all law enforcers were government agents such as FBI agent Bill Maxwell on *The Greatest American Hero.* The remaining 1 percent were included in a residual category represented by such professions as security guards.

Most private eyes (69 percent) were series stars while a majority of both lawyers and government agents made only a single appearance. When police appeared they were most likely to be minor series regulars (49 percent), while 29 percent were stars and 22 percent made a single appearance.

Law enforcers on television were predominantly white males in the prime of life. Eighty-nine percent were male and nearly as many (85 percent) were white. The remaining

15 percent were black. No other non-white groups were represented. Sixty-three percent were between the ages of 30 and 50, while the rest were about equally divided between those under 30 and those over 50.

Most law enforcers were one-dimensional characters whose roles revolved around getting their job done. Two out of three were shown engaging in purely occupational tasks. By contrast, only 6 percent were featured in a personal role and 27 percent combined elements of their work and personal lives. Some shows did present the private lives of law enforcers. For example, in an episode of *Soap* a police officer and his girlfriend argue about the seriousness of their relationship (3/16). But such cases are rare. Viewers are much more likely to see private detective *Nero Wolfe* solving a crime or police captain *Barney Miller* juggling the problems of fellow officers and New York City residents.

Stars, whose characterizations have the best chance to be well developed on TV, were more likely to involve themselves in varied activities than were other types of characters. They were about twice as likely to engage in personal activities or to combine occupational and personal tasks, as were minor regulars or single-appearance characters.

Private eyes, the group most likely to be starts, also had the greatest chance at a more well-rounded role. Thus, private eye Dan Tanna of *Vegas* stalks the murderer of a woman to whom he had a deep personal attachment (4/1).

In general, however, strictly law-related activities consumed most of these characters' time. Perhaps this is why the audience received very little information on their economic status. Eighty-nine percent of all law enforcers were of unknown economic status. Three percent were wealthy, 8 percent middle class and none were working class or poor.

Plot Functions

The most crucial aspect of the law enforcer's role deals with the general nature of his function. Were law enforcers the dedicated protectors of justice or were they themselves lawbreakers? Did they possess the skills to execute their jobs properly or did crimes go unsolved due to their incompetence?

In general, law enforcers fared well although they were somewhat tainted by incompetence or even illegal behavior. Table 15 shows that 54 percent were portrayed positively, 28 percent negatively and 18 percent played neutral roles. Representative of the positively portrayed law enforcers was Sheriff Lobo from the show of the same name. In one segment, for instance, he works out a plan to capture bank robbers who had taken a group of customers hostage (4/7). By contrast, a sheriff of less noble motives, Titus Simple of *Flamingo Road,* is involved in blackmailing and bribery (4/2). Typical of the neutral law enforcers is an attorney on *Nero Wolfe* who briefly discusses a case with the series star (3/6).

Although this general picture of law enforcers held true for both comedies and dramas, there were differences on the three networks, indicated by Table 16. Those on ABC and NBC were positive a majority of the time (62 and 56 percent respectively), but on CBS negative law enforcers slightly outnumbered positive ones (39 to 37 percent). ABC painted a somewhat rosier picture than the other two networks, casting only 15 percent of its law enforcers as bad guys.

Many other characteristics were involved in the portrayal of a character's plot function. For example, as Table 17 shows, stars fared much better than other types of characters. An overwhelming majority of stars (80 percent) were positive compared to 50 percent for minor series regulars and a mere 32 percent for those making guest shots. These single-appearance characters fared worst of all—38 percent were shown as bad guys. Minor continuing characters were close behind with a 31 percent negative rating. In contrast, only 14 percent of stars were cast as bad guys.

Among the majority of stars making a brave showing are police officers Baker and Poncherello of *CHiPs* who try to protect a man from the threats of his deranged enemy (4/5). Minor regulars, who are usually portrayed positively as well, include a police detective on *Hill Street Blues* who goes un-

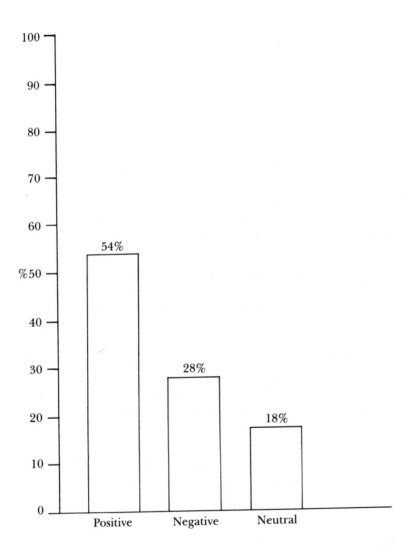

Table 15. Plot Functions of Law Enforcers. (%)

Table 16. Plot Functions of Law Enforcers by Network. (%)

Function	ABC	NBC	CBS
Positive	62	56	37
Negative	17	30	39
Neutral	21	14	24
	100%	100%	100%
Number of Cases	99	203	71

dercover in an attempt to capture a drug dealer (3/21). Among single-appearance characters (who do not fare as well) is a gruff police detective on *Different Strokes* who arrests an innocent woman on theft charges (4/1).

Younger and nonwhite law enforcers also fared better than others. We see from Table 18 that 68 percent of those under 30 were portrayed positively compared to 53 percent for those aged 30 to 50 and 40 percent for those over 50. Those in the older age groups were almost three times as likely to be bad guys as were the young law enforcers. Thus, a police detective approaching retirement on *Hill Street Blues* helps cover up a politician's involvement in a young girl's murder (3/21).

Among nonwhite law enforcers, as Table 19 shows, 64 percent of portrayals were positive compared to 52 percent among whites. Even more striking, whites were more than twice as likely to be portrayed negatively (31 vs. 13 percent.)

Table 17. Plot Functions of Law Enforcers by Type of Role. (%)

Function	Star	Minor Regular	Single Appearance
Positive	80	51	32
Negative	14	31	38
Neutral	6	18	30
	100%	100%	100%
Number of Cases	112	152	109

Table 18. Plot Functions of Law Enforcers By Age. (%)

Function	Under 30	30–50	Over 50
Positive	68	53	40
Negative	13	31	34
Neutral	19	16	26
	100%	100%	100%
Number of Cases	74	237	62

Some types of law enforcers also made a better showing than others. The differences are shown in Table 20. The positive image of private eyes far outstripped all other groups. Ninety-three percent of these one-man guardians of justice were shown favorably, and not a single character was a bad guy. The remaining 7 percent played neutral roles. Otherwise they were a varied lot. Among their ranks was the portly *Nero Wolfe,* young and stylish Dan Tanna of *Vegas* and tough Thomas Magnum from *Magnum, P.I.*

Police were the next most favorably portrayed group. A slight majority of 53 percent played positive roles, 30 percent were negative and 17 percent neutral. Typical of positive images of police was Dan Tanna's friend, the dedicated Lieutenant Dave Nelson of *Vegas.* Negative police were more likely to resemble a vicious and corrupt captain on *BJ and the Bear* who accepts bribes and is involved in drug deals (4/14, 3/24).

Table 19. Plot Functions of Law Enforcers by Race. (%)

Function	White	Nonwhite
Positive	52	64
Negative	31	13
Neutral	17	23
	100%	100%
Number of Cases	318	55

Table 20. Plot Functions of Law Enforcers by Occupation. (%)

Function	Police	Lawyer
Positive	53	44
Negative	30	31
Neutral	17	25
	100%	100%
Number of Cases	263	64

	Private Investigator	Government Agent
Positive	93	40
Negative	0	40
Neutral	7	20
	100%	100%
Number of Cases	29	15

Lawyers fared somewhat less well than policemen although a plurality was portrayed in a favorable light. Forty-four percent received positive portrayals, 31 percent were shown as negative and the remaining 25 percent played neutral roles. They ranged from admirable characters like Joyce Davenport, the tireless public defender (and Captain Furillo's love interest) on *Hill Street Blues*, to shysters and worse. In fact, several ended up on the wrong side of the law, like a lawyer on *Nero Wolfe* who is responsible for a murder (4/17).

Government agents were the only major group with as many negative as positive portrayals: 40 percent on each side of the ledger. Even the good guys were rarely of the square-jawed heroic variety. More representative was Bill Maxwell of *The Greatest American Hero,* a competent but unpolished FBI agent. This group was just as likely to include such characters as an incompetent CIA agent who is too concerned with agency red tape to notice the clues to a kidnapping (*The Greatest American Hero*—4/8).

The portraits of these law enforcers become more revealing when we examine the particular types of positive and negative functions they performed. Law enforcers were more likely to be positive than negative, but when they did err their transgressions were fairly serious as Table 21 illustrates. Twenty-nine percent of the bad guys committed illegal acts and an equal number were professionally incompetent. Eighteen percent were foolish, an equal number were greedy and the remaining 6 percent were malevolent.

Moreover, as Table 22 reveals, different types of law enforcers were guilty of quite different patterns of negative behavior. Lawyers who erred were most likely to be greedy (40 percent) and least likely to be professionally incompetent (10 percent). In contrast, police usually committed a crime themselves (33 percent) or failed to perform their jobs competently (32 percent). Half the bad government agents were incompetent and a third were greedy. Among law enforcers who turned to crime is a police sergeant on *Enos* who deals in drugs (4/15). In a demonstration of occupational incompetence, an officer on *Hill Street Blues* exacerbates an argument between two men involved in a fender-bender by losing his own temper (4/4).

We see from Table 23 that positive law enforcers were a more uniform lot. Two-thirds of them (65 percent) demonstrated professional competence, 27 percent were friendly or helpful and 8 percent went beyond the call of duty.

The critical differences among the types of positive acts performed were reflected in the different types of characters and occupations. First, as Table 24 indicates, stars were most likely to be competent or heroic. Seventy-two percent of stars who were positively portrayed performed their jobs well, compared to 65 percent of minor series regulars and 51 percent of those making a guest appearance. Both minor characters and guests were more likely to be merely friendly than were stars. Fifteen percent of these stars performed some heroic deed compared to only 1 percent of minor regulars and 3 percent of single-appearance characters.

Overall, stars were responsible for 87 percent of heroic acts performed by law enforcers. Among these heroes was

Table 21. Types of Negative Functions Performed
by Law Enforcers. (%)

29%	6%	18%	18%	29%
Illegal	Malevolent	Foolish	Greedy	Incompetent

100

40

%30

20

10

0

Table 22. Types of Negative Behavior by Occupation. (%)

Behavior	Police	Lawyer	Government Agent
Illegal	33	20	17
Malevolent	4	15	0
Foolish	19	15	0
Greedy	12	40	33
Incompetent	32	10	50
	100%	100%	100%
Number of Cases	78	20	6

police captain Frank Furillo of *Hill Street Blues* who not only negotiates to save a group of hostages from sure death but uses his personal time and connections to have a misguided juvenile placed in a private rehabilitation center (4/21). In another example of heroism, police captain Barney Miller refuses to divulge the identity of an informant and goes to jail to preserve the credibility of his department (3/19).

Of lawyers who were positive, half were friendly and half were competent. Eighty-three percent of government agents were competent and 17 percent (only one case) heroic. Among police about two-thirds were competent, 27 percent friendly and 8 percent heroic. Private eyes were mostly competent (82 percent) with 11 friendly and 7 percent heroic.

Finally, Table 25 combines all the various positive and negative functions into a single comparison to provide an overview of how law enforcement is portrayed on prime-time television. The most frequent portrayal was one of simple competence. Over one in three characters who enforce the law were shown doing their jobs adequately if not heroically. Only 4 percent, or one in 25, acted beyond the call of duty. For that is the flip side of television's emphasis on the competent cop (or other law enforcer). In fact, for every law enforcer who performed heroically, two performed incompetently and another two actually broke the

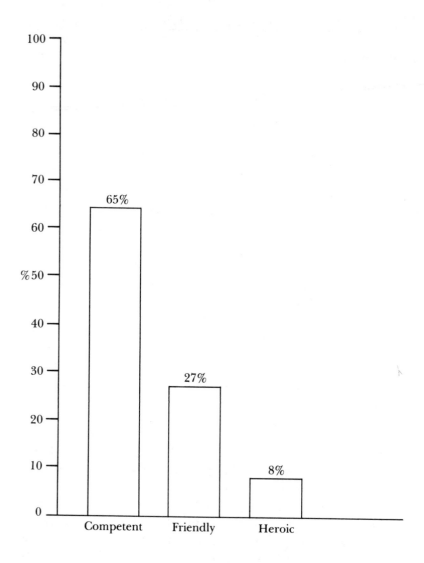

Table 23. Types of Positive Functions Performed
by Law Enforcers. (%)

Table 24. Types of Positive Behavior by Role in a Series. (%)

Behavior	Star	Minor Regular	Single Appearance
Competent	72	65	51
Friendly	13	34	46
Heroic	15	1	3
	100%	100%	100%
Number of Cases	89	77	35

law themselves. Incompetence and illegal activity each accounted for one characterization in 12 among law enforcement characters. To be sure, both categories were outweighed by competent characters as well as those who behaved in a friendly or otherwise sympathetic fashion. As we noted earlier, positive portrayals far outweighed negative ones. But equally noteworthy was the dearth of heroes among a group whose occupations make them prime candidates for any number of heroic scenarios.

Bending The Rules

Beyond simple plot function, we examined other aspects of the way law enforcers performed their duties. We were interested in characters who bend the rules to get the job done. The unorthodox defender of justice who rarely does things according to "the book" is a stock entertainment device. Such characters conform to the spirit but not the letter of the law and they often have to fight the system in order to make it work.

This tradition is at least as old as Sherlock Holmes and as contemporary as *Baretta* and *Kojak*. Thus, we analyzed current portrayals of law enforcers with this time-honored theme in mind. Specifically, in upholding both the law and principles of justice, do law enforcers themselves "bend the rules" in the greater pursuit of justice? If so, how far do they bend the rules and how does this affect their portrayal on television?

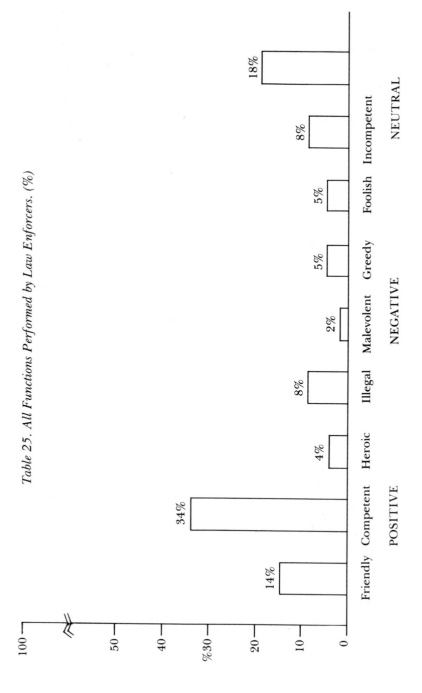

Table 25. All Functions Performed by Law Enforcers. (%)

We found that a relatively small part of the sample, only 8 percent, bent the rules for any reason while remaining on the side of the angels. On the light side, such behavior included two *Hill Street Blues* police officers who appropriate for their barbecue a bullet-ridden side of beef that was to be used as evidence (4/21). On the same series, a dedicated police detective becomes overly enthusiastic during an interrogation and bites the ankle of an assailant. He is quickly lectured by his superior, Frank Furillo, on preserving criminals' rights and he promises not to repeat such behavior (3/28).

Among other unorthodox law enforcers, private eye Dan Tanna of *Vegas* searches a hotel room to find information on a murderer (4/1). FBI man Bill Maxwell of *The Greatest American Hero* is an accessory to "borrowing" FBI files concerning a case in which he is entwined (4/8).

In a more serious vein, sheriff Bufford Pusser from the short-lived series *Walking Tall* bursts into a building without a warrant and destroys the equipment for a drug making operation (3/31).

Those who did bend the rules were most likely to be stars (47 percent), and the two groups of series regulars together constituted 87 percent of the rule bending. Interestingly, these rule benders fared somewhat better as a group than those who walked a straight line. Of those who bent the rules, 64 percent were portrayed positively compared to a 56 percent positive rating for those who went by the book. Government agents were more than twice as likely as any other occupational group to bend the rules; 20 percent did so. But this total was largely accounted for by the repeated escapades of Bill Maxwell, the not-so-typical FBI man on *The Greatest American Hero*.

Solving Crimes

We usually think of crime solving as the chief business of law enforcers—pursuing criminals rather than tending to more mundane activities certainly makes for more exciting television. Surprisingly, however, almost half of all law enforcers (49 percent) were not involved in crime-solving ac-

Table 26. Crime-Solving Activity by Plot Function. (%)

Function	Solves	Assists	Fails	Not Involved
Positive	98	84	27	38
Negative	1	14	49	35
Neutral	1	2	24	27
	100%	100%	100%	100%
Number of Cases	75	49	66	183

ity even if they performed other tasks related to their jobs. Twenty percent were primary agents in solving crimes and 13 percent lent secondary assistance in this endeavor. Eighteen percent of those involved in tracking criminals failed to solve crimes.

Involvement in crime solving varied considerably among the different types of characters. Forty-nine percent of all stars were primary agents in solving crimes compared to only 5 percent among minor regulars and 11 percent of those making guest appearances. Only 5 percent of stars failed at solving crimes compared to 24 percent of minor series regulars and 22 percent of guest characters.

A character's role in crime-solving was closely linked with his overall function. Table 26 shows that 98 percent of the primary crime-solving agents were positively portrayed as were 84 percent of secondary agents. In contrast, only 38 percent of those not involved in crime solving were shown as positive, as were only 27 percent of those who were involved in investigations but did not solve the crime. Forty-nine percent of those in the last group were shown in a negative light.

Dexterity in solving crimes was also related to a law enforcer's occupation as Table 27 indicates. The key finding here was the high success rate of private eyes relative to all other groups. Sixty-two percent of the private eyes were portrayed as catching the bad guy themselves, a success rate over three times as high as that enjoyed by any other group.

Table 27. Crime-Solving Activity by Occupation. (%)

Role in Solving Crime	Police	Lawyer
Solves	19	3
Assists	14	3
Fails	21	8
Not Involved	46	86
	100%	100%
Number of Cases	263	64

	Private Investigator	Government Agent
Solves	62	20
Assists	28	14
Fails	7	33
Not Involved	3	33
	100%	100%
Number of Cases	29	15

By contrast, only 19 percent of policemen functioned as primary crime solvers.

Thus, the role of private eyes like Dan Tanna, Thomas Magnum and Nero Wolfe usually focused on crime solving. Even when other law enforcers assisted them, these private eyes inevitably ended up in the Sherlock Holmes role as master crime solver, while their companions were relegated to the role of second-rate Doctor Watsons.

The privileged position of private eyes helped mask most law enforcers' tendency to fail at crime solving. Every other group actually failed to get its man more often than it succeeded. By contrast, private eyes proved almost incapable of failure in catching criminals; the 7 percent who did so paled in comparison to the 62 percent who were primary agents in solving crimes.

The unexpectedly high failure rate of most law enforcers, combined with the fantastic success of private eyes, is one of

Table 28. Crime-Solving Activity by Plot Resolution. (%)

Resolution	Solve	Assist	Fail	Not Involved
Success	95	87	32	34
Defeat	0	2	48	32
Character Change	0	2	7	2
Unresolved	5	9	13	32
	100%	100%	100%	100%
Number of Cases	73	47	44	122

the most striking findings of the study. Once again it is the outsider—the man in the trenchcoat—who saves the day when ordinary law enforcers prove unequal to the task.

Plot Resolution

The involvement in crime solving (along with a host of other factors) affected the way characters fared in plot resolution. The results are shown in Table 28. Not surprisingly, 95 percent of the primary crime solvers and 87 percent of the secondary ones were ultimately successful compared to only about a third of those who were either not involved in crime solving or those who were involved but did not solve a crime themselves. The latter groups were defeated 32 and 48 percent of the time respectively.

Overall, law enforcers succeeded 58 percent of the time and were defeated 21 percent of the time. Two percent underwent a character change and 19 percent had an unresolved outcome.

Not surprisingly, stars (who were more likely to be positive and primary crime solvers) were also the most successful. As Table 29 indicates, 76 percent of all stars were successful compared to 59 percent of minor regulars and 31 percent of those who made a single appearance. This last group was the only one more likely to be defeated than to succeed. Thirty-seven percent of these guest characters were defeated compared to 25 percent of minor regulars

Table 29. Plot Resolution by Character's Role in a Series. (%)

Resolution	Star	Minor Regular	Single Appearance
Success	76	59	31
Defeat	5	25	37
Character Change	1	3	4
Unresolved	18	13	28
	100%	100%	100%
Number of Cases	73	47	122

and only 5 percent of stars. Among the successful stars was Sheriff Lobo who captures bank robbers and rescues those they had held hostage (4/7). Likewise, a police detective who played a minor continuing role on *Hill Street Blues* succeeds in capturing a drug dealer (4/4). But among single appearance law enforcers, a police sergeant on *Enos* who deals in drugs is himself captured by other police (4/15).

Overall, success was enjoyed by positively portrayed law enforcers while evil or foolish ones were defeated. Eighty-five percent of positive characters were successful and only 4 percent were defeated. The remainder was unresolved. In contrast, 59 percent of the bad guys failed and only 10 percent succeeded.

Differences in outcome were also evident among various occupations, as Table 30 reveals. Private eyes received the lion's share of success with a 100 percent success rate in plot resolutions. This diminished to 59 percent for police, 34 percent for lawyers and 33 percent for government agents. This last group was defeated twice as often as it succeeded while police and lawyers were each defeated about 20 percent of the time.

Typical of private investigators was Dan Tanna who miraculously captures a murderer even though he is temporarily blinded (3/18). In contrast, a police detective on *Hill Street Blues* ignores all of his other responsibilities because he wants to set up a laundromat on the side. But his hopes and

Table 30. Plot Resolution by Occupation. (%)

Resolution	Police	Lawyer	Private Investigator	Government Agent
Success	59	34	100	33
Defeat	22	20	0	67
Character Change	3	4	0	0
Unresolved	16	42	0	0
	100%	100%	100%	100%
Number of Cases	195	50	28	12

financial investment are dissolved when the property he purchases for his business is destroyed (3/21). And of course the most egregious of bad guys, like a drug dealing cop on *Enos,* gets a taste of the law and order he fails to uphold (4/15).

Citizens In Law Enforcement

Thus far we have dealt only with characters who are law enforcers by profession. But on television, citizens play an active role in crime solving. Here we shall document their role and examine how these citizens relate to law enforcers in the fight against crime.

A total of 37 citizens took some active part in crime solving in the series we coded. They accounted for just under 10 percent of all characters involved in law enforcement. Many did so because the crimes somehow affected them or their acquaintances. For example, millionaire Jonathan Hart of *Hart to Hart* cracks a counterfeiting ring that was operating on a ship he owned (4/14).

Relative to the law enforcement professionals, citizens were more likely to be stars. Eighty-one percent of them were series stars like Jonathan and Jennifer Hart or the hell-raising Duke boys from *The Dukes of Hazzard.* Among professional law enforcers, private eyes were most likely to be stars (69 percent).

Citizens were also more positively portrayed than other law enforcement characters. In fact, all citizens involved in solving crimes were shown positively. The most positively portrayed law enforcers were private eyes, another group of "outsiders," at 93 percent. But from there it is quite a drop to the 53 percent positive rating for police.

Thirty percent of citizens bent the rules—a higher proportion than any group of law enforcers. But this did not tarnish their positive image at all. Thus, a high school teacher who leads a double life as *The Greatest American Hero* "flies" into the FBI to "borrow" files on a top-secret case (4/8). And hero Jonathan Hart breaks into an apartment to find information on a murderer (3/17).

Further, citizens were more likely to be primary crime solvers than any group of law enforcers. Sixty-eight percent were primary crime solvers, as were 62 percent of private eyes. Yet only 20 percent of police and 19 percent of government agents were the primary solvers.

Not surprisingly, almost all citizens (97 percent) were successful in their endeavor. Only PIs enjoyed a slightly higher success rate of 100 percent in plot resolutions. This was quite a contrast to the next-highest success rate of 59 percent for police. Thus, Jonathan Hart captures a murderer (3/24) and breaks up a counterfeiting ring (4/14) while *The Greatest American Hero* saves a young couple from the clutches of Soviet spies (4/8).

V. Summary and Conclusions

For every American who is victimized by crime, several experience crime vicariously each evening on their television sets. But while cops and robbers are a staple of TV entertainment, we know very little about how TV portrays crime and the law.

In this study we examined the nature of crime and law enforcement portrayed in 263 prime-time programs from the 1980–81 television season. We employed a content analysis system to analyze the types of illegal behavior shown, the characteristics of criminals, and the portrayal of law enforcement officials on these programs.

Prime-time television creates a fantasy world that is frequently dangerous and violent. Our study identified 417 illegal acts, an average of about 1.7 crimes per series episode. Moreover, lawbreakers on television tended to engage in the most serious and violent crimes to an extent that bears little relation to reality. Every fourth crime shown was a murder; one crime in six was a violent theft. Overall, a majority of all illegal acts portrayed were crimes of violence.

Television introduces the viewer to two types of criminals—the professional deviant who lives a life of crime, and the apparent pillar of the community who turns to crime to maintain or better his standard of living. Criminals on prime time are usually middle- or upper-class white males over age 30. As "mature" adults, they rarely act on impulse. Instead their lawbreaking is carefully calculated to advance their own interest.

The vast majority of television crime is predicated on pure

greed. Wealthy characters are over twice as likely to commit crimes as those identified as poor or middle class. Along these lines, a stock criminal type is the businessman whose selfish pursuit of profit leads him into illegal activity. TV businessmen and their underlings account for almost one in four lawbreakers with identifiable occupations—they constitute the largest criminal group aside from professional gangsters. But substantial numbers of criminals are other pillars of the community, including educated professionals and the police themselves. In fact, one television criminal in eight is drawn from the ranks of those sworn to uphold the law.

Of course, all this is only half the story. Criminals on television are vigorously pursued and usually thwarted by a variety of crime stoppers. We identified 373 characters as law enforcers. Over two-thirds were police, with the remainder divided among private eyes, lawyers, judges and government agents. An additional 37 private citizens performed law enforcement functions, such as capturing the criminal.

Law enforcers appeared frequently on comedies and dramas alike, on all three networks, in both continuing and single-appearance roles. Most were white males; 15 percent were nonwhites; and 11 percent were women.

In general, law enforcers were portrayed in a positive light although "supercops" were rarely seen. Fifty-four percent functioned as good guys, 28 percent as villains, and the rest played neutral roles. The largest number, about one in three, was portrayed as doing their job in a competent manner. However, very few were cast in a heroic light—only 4 percent went beyond the call of duty rather than just performing competently. Moreover, significant percentages were portrayed as either inept or positively criminal; about one law enforcer in 12 fell into these categories. Thus, law enforcers fared rather well in general, but they were tainted somewhat by incompetence and even illegal behavior.

A major finding was the privileged position of private investigators relative to all other groups of law enforcers. Ninety-three percent of private eyes functioned as good guys, compared to 53 percent of police and fewer than half the lawyers and government agents. In all the programs we viewed not a single private eye played the heavy. By contrast, the crooked cop and the greedy lawyer provided recurring negative images of law enforcers.

Private eyes proved almost godlike in their crime-solving abilities, while other law enforcers were often portrayed as mere mortals. Sixty-two percent of the private eyes were the primary agents in solving crimes, compared to only 19 percent of policemen. In fact, every group other than private eyes failed to solve crimes more often than they succeeded, though they sometimes assisted others in making the collar. By contrast, private eyes succeeded almost nine times as often as they failed.

The phenomenal success of private eyes was part of a broader trend involving the need for outside help or unorthodox means to enforce the law. In addition to that quintessential outsider, the private eye, the police often required the help of private citizens to foil the bad guys. Their assistance did not take the form of providing evidence or identifying suspects, but of actually solving the crime themselves. Private citizens actually edged out private eyes as the most effective group of crime solvers. Finally, law enforcers who bent the rules were over twice as likely to solve crimes as those who went by the book.

This portrait of crime and law enforcement is perhaps most notable for what it fails to show about the crime problem that today preoccupies the American public. Television entertainment largely ignores most aspects of real crime in America, focusing instead on the most serious, violent and life-threatening offenses. By sensationalizing crime in this way, TV misses its opportunity to educate the audience about the true dimensions of America's crime problem. Television's nightly stream of murder, mugging and mayhem obscures the less dramatic but much more common threats to law-abiding citizens from such unspectacular sources as drunkenness, drug abuse and larceny.

If prime-time crime bears little relation to the genuine article, television's criminals are equally far removed from their real-life counterparts. The main focus is on the avarice of the middle and upper classes. We rarely see the juvenile delinquent or the youth gang. Nor are we exposed to the culture of poverty that is directly or indirectly responsible for so much crime. Similarly, the black community's increasing public concern with street crime is rarely in evidence.

For all the criminal activity, in one respect there is no crime "problem" on television. In the fantasy world of TV entertainment (unlike the real world) most lawbreakers are thwarted and crime is punished—yet ordinary law enforcement officials are presented as highly fallible. More often than not, they either fail to catch the crook or they play supporting roles for the heroic private eyes who are television's real crime stoppers.

Neither Dick Tracy nor Joe Friday serves as the model law enforcer for today's cops-and-robbers shows. We found few square-jawed *Blue Knights* who capture the villains and comfort the victims. Nor does television favor the methodical and mundane investigative style of *Dragnet's* dedicated cops. Instead, the glamor boy of TV's legal system is the private eye, whose Holmesian abilities often consign the law enforcement professionals to the role of Doctor Watson.

More broadly, effective law enforcement is often the province of the outsider who bypasses the law enforcement establishment. On television, the police, the government and the legal profession are often shown as competent if uninspired upholders of the law. But these law enforcement professionals often need the help of the lone outsider—the private eye or the citizen-detective—to bring evildoers to justice.

In sum, the artificial world of prime time is a dangerous and crime-ridden place. Evildoers are drawn from the ranks of both professional criminals and apparent pillars of the community. Most are thwarted before the final credits, but policemen are rarely the heroes. Television manages to enforce the law without glorifying the law enforcement establishment. Surprisingly often on prime time, the insiders break the law and the outsiders enforce it.

VI. Appendices

Appendix A: Crime and Criminals

The following programs were coded for crime and criminals:

ABC

Hart to Hart
Mar. 3, '81
Mar. 10, '81
Mar. 24, '81
Apr. 14, '81
Apr. 21, '81

Vegas
Mar. 4, '81
Mar. 11, '81
Mar. 18, '81
Mar. 25, '81
Apr. 1, '81
Apr. 15, '81

*The Greatest
American Hero*
Mar. 18, '81

Apr. 8, '81
Apr. 15, '81
Sept. 30, '81

240-Robert
Mar. 21, '81

Soap
Mar. 9, '81
Mar. 16, '81
Apr. 20, '81

Taxi
Apr. 16, '81

I'm a Big Girl Now
Apr. 10, '81

Three's Company
Apr. 14, '81

Benson
Mar. 13, '81

Dynasty
Mar. 9, '81

Fantasy Island
Mar. 28, '81
Apr. 18, '81

Barney Miller
Mar. 12, '81
Mar. 19, '81
Mar. 26, '81
Apr. 2, '81
Apr. 16, '81

Mork and Mindy
Apr. 16, '81

NBC

Facts of Life
Apr. 15, '81
Sheriff Lobo
Mar. 3, '81
Mar. 10, '81
Mar. 24, '81
Apr. 7, '81
Apr. 21, '81
Nero Wolfe
Mar. 6, '81
Mar. 20, '81
Mar. 27, '81
Apr. 10, '81
Apr. 17, '81
Hill Street Blues
Mar. 21, '81
Mar. 25, '81
Mar. 28, '81
Apr. 4, '81
Apr. 21, '81

Walking Tall
Mar. 24, '81
Mar. 31, '81
Apr. 7, '81
CHiPs
Mar. 29, '81
Apr. 5, '81
Apr. 19, '81
Sept. 13, '81
Flamingo Road
Mar. 3, '81
Mar. 10, '81
Mar. 17, '81
Apr. 2, '81

BJ and the Bear
Mar. 10, '81
Mar. 17, '81
Mar. 24, '81
Mar. 31, '81
Apr. 7, '81
Apr. 14, '81
Gangster Chronicles
Mar. 21, '81
Apr. 22, '81
Quincy
Apr. 8, '81

CBS

Magnum, P.I.
Mar. 19, '81
Mar. 26, '81
Apr. 2, '81
Apr. 16, '81
Apr. 23, '81
Palmerstown, U.S.A.
Mar. 31, '81
Apr. 14, '81
Apr. 21, '81
Trapper John, M.D.
Sept. 6, '81
White Shadow
Mar. 2, '81
Nurse
Sept. 30, '81

The Jeffersons
Mar. 29, '81
House Calls
Mar. 16, '81
Apr. 6, '81
Knots Landing
Mar. 26, '81
Dukes of Hazzard
Mar. 13, '81
Mar. 20, '81
Mar. 27, '81
Apr. 3, '81
Apr. 10, '81
Apr. 17, '81

The Incredible Hulk
Mar. 6, '81
Lou Grant
Mar. 16, '81
Enos
Mar. 18, '81
Apr. 1, '81
Apr. 15, '81

Appendix B: Law Enforcers

The following programs were coded for law enforcers:

ABC

The Greatest American Hero
Mar. 18, '81
Apr. 8, '81
Apr. 15, '81
Sept. 30, '81

Vegas
Mar. 4, '81
Mar. 11, '81
Mar. 18, '81
Mar. 25, '81
Apr. 1, '81
Apr. 15, '81

Hart to Hart
Mar. 3, '81
Mar. 10, '81
Mar. 17, '81
Mar. 24, '81
Apr. 14, '81
Apr. 21, '81

Fantasy Island
Mar. 28, '81
Apr. 18, '81

Three's Company
Apr. 14, '81

Soap
Mar. 9, '81
Mar. 16, '81
Apr. 20, '81

I'm a Big Girl Now
Mar. 20, '81

Mork and Mindy
Apr. 16, '81

Dynasty
Mar. 9, '81
Apr. 20, '81

Taxi
Apr. 16, '81

Aloha Paradise
Apr. 15, '81

Benson
Mar. 13, '81
Apr. 10, '81

240-Robert
Mar. 21, '81

NBC

Quincy
Mar. 4, '81
Mar. 11, '81
Apr. 1, '81
Apr. 8, '81

BJ and the Bear
Mar. 10, '81
Mar. 17, '81
Mar. 24, '81
Mar. 31, '81
Apr. 7, '81
Apr. 14, '81

Nero Wolfe
Mar. 6, '81
Mar. 20, '81
Mar. 27, '81
Apr. 10, '81
Apr. 17, '81

Sheriff Lobo
Mar. 3, '81
Mar. 10, '81
Mar. 24, '81
Apr. 7, '81
Apr. 21, '81

Hill Street Blues
Mar. 21, '81
Mar. 25, '81
Mar. 28, '81
Apr. 4, '81
Apr. 21, '81

Walking Tall
Mar. 24, '81
Mar. 31, '81
Apr. 7, '81

CHiPs
Mar. 24, '81
Apr. 5, '81
Apr. 19, '81
Sept. 13, '81
Little House on the Prairie
Mar. 9, '81

Harper Valley P.T.A.
Mar. 6, '81
Mar. 20, '81
Mar. 27, '81
Apr. 17, '81
Flamingo Road
Mar. 3, '81
Mar. 10, '81
Mar. 17, '81
Apr. 2, '81

Gangster Chronicles
Mar. 21, '81
Apr. 22, '81
Facts of Life
Apr. 15, '81
Brady Brides
Mar. 27, '81

CBS

Magnum, P.I.
Mar. 19, '81
Mar. 26, '81
Apr. 2, '81
Apr. 16, '81
Apr. 23, '81
White Shadow
Mar. 2, '81
Mar. 16, '81
Enos
Mar. 18, '81
Apr. 1, '81
Apr. 15, '81
Dukes of Hazzard
Mar. 13, '81
Mar. 20, '81
Mar. 27, '81
Apr. 3, '81
Apr. 10, '81
Apr. 17, '81

The Jeffersons
Mar. 29, '81
Palmerstown, U.S.A.
Mar. 31, '81
Apr. 14, '81
Apr. 21, '81
House Calls
Mar. 2, '81
Mar. 9, '81
Trapper John, M.D.
Sept. 6, '81
The Waltons
Mar. 19, '81
The Incredible Hulk
Mar. 6, '81
One Day at a Time
Sept. 20, '81

Park Place
Apr. 16, '81
Lou Grant
Mar. 16, '81
Apr. 13, '81
Archie Bunker's Place
Mar. 29, '81
Sept. 20, '81
Dallas
Mar. 27, '81
Apr. 3, '81
Apr. 10, '81
Apr. 17, '81